BRAIN BOOSTERS
MATH PUZZLES

ARCTURUS

ARCTURUS

This edition published in 2018 by Arcturus Publishing Limited
26/27 Bickels Yard, 151–153 Bermondsey Street,
London SE1 3HA

ISBN: 978-1-78828-501-8
CH005806NT
Supplier 29, Date 0718, Print run 7741

Written by Lisa Regan
Illustrated by Samantha Meredith with Ed Myers and Graham Rich
Designed by Trudi Webb

Printed in China

TIPS ON SOLVING PUZZLES FROM A WISE OLD BIRD

Here are some wise words to help you on your way.

Some of the puzzles are just about counting. Keep your cool and have fun.

Certain puzzles require you to see patterns in numbers. Think carefully about the sequences you see.

Write everything down to check that your calculations are correct.

If you get stuck on a problem involving adding, subtracting, multiplication, or division, try using a calculator.

RACE AGAINST TIME

Sanjay starts his sand sculpture at 1.30pm. Each dragon takes him 45 minutes, and a castle takes an hour and twenty minutes. How long will the completed sculpture be on show? Sadly, the tide washes it all away at half past six.

PARKING SPACE

There is room in each garage for three cars or two trucks. Cars and trucks cannot share the same garage. How many of these vehicles will have to park elsewhere?

Best in show

Each rabbit has been given a number. Which numbered rabbits have won prizes?

1

2

3

4

5

6

7

8

9

10

The gold cup winner can be divided by 2 and 4 and is >6.

The red rosette goes to the largest multiple of 5.

The orange rosette winner is 21 ÷ 3.

MONSTER MUNCH

Help the monster chomp its way through a total of 60,
without retracing its steps at any point.

T-SHIRT TRENDS

Study the designs on these T-shirts, and then work out the answers to the questions.

1. How many stars do you predict there will be on the sixth shirt in the collection?
2. And how many stars on the 100th T-shirt?
3. Will the 22nd shirt have long sleeves or short sleeves?
4. What number of spots do you predict will appear on the 30th T-shirt?

SNACK TIME

Each creature in this food pyramid eats ten of the thing below it. How many frogs must 10 snakes eat? Fill in the missing numbers.

1 eagle

10 snakes

_ _ _ frogs

_ _ _ _ crickets

_ _ _ _ _ blades of grass

9

Sail away

The passengers must solve the problems on their tickets to see which ship they should board. Which ship has the fewest passengers?

38

39

40

78 x 0.5

19 + 19

120 x 1/3

(16 x 2) + 8

76 ÷ 2

80 – (21 x 2)

13 x 3

(90 x 0.5) – 5

HUNGRY GAMES

If 6 caterpillars can eat 60 leaves in an hour, how long would it take for 8 caterpillars to eat 40 leaves?

11

GIFT WRAPPED

Which of the shapes below folds into the box that Stacey's present came in?

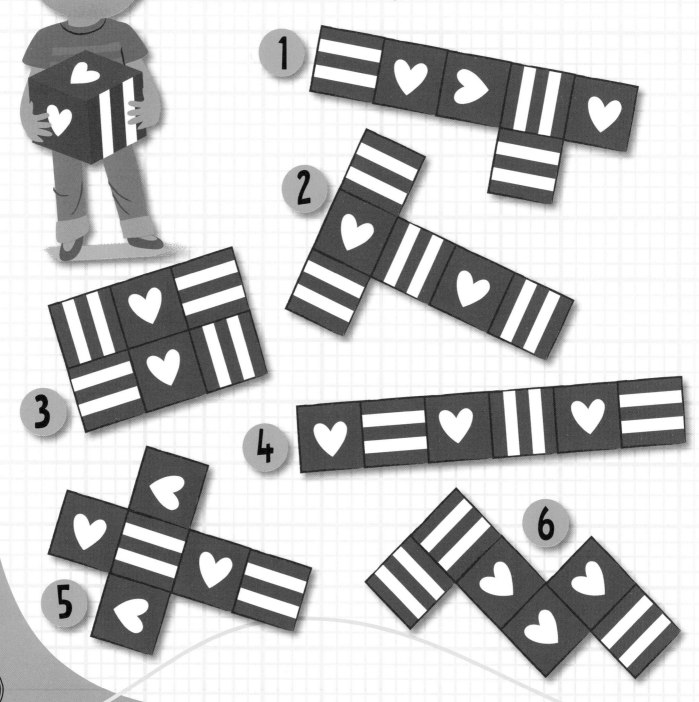

Penny has put her toy cars into boxes. Some cars are green, some are yellow, and some are blue. Can you work out what the probability is of taking a green car from each box? The first has been done to show you how.

TOY CARS

1 In a box containing 1 blue and 1 green, the probability of picking a green car is 1/2.

2 In a box containing 3 blue and 1 green, the probability of picking a green car is ___

3 In a box containing 6 yellow and 4 green, the probability of picking a green car is ___

4 In a box containing 2 blue, 2 yellow, and 2 green, the probability of picking a green car is ___

5 In a box containing 3 green, 3 blue, and 6 yellow, the probability of picking a green car is ___

Which of the number blocks is not needed to finish the pyramid? Each block shows the sum of the two blocks propping it up.

52

13 | 11

7 | 4 | 6

Number blocks: 44, 26, 23, 10, 29, 96, 5, 9, 21, 16

Deck the halls

a 5 1 6 3 5 4

b 5 6 4 1 3 6

c 2 4 5 3 2 1

d 1 3 2 6 4 2

The members of the Number Club are decorating their clubhouse. They want each banner to have six different numbers. Make one cut in each banner and retie the strings so that no banner has the same number twice.

15

SNEAKY SNACKS

Each snack is worth a different number. When they are added across or down, they equal the total in the circle. What snack is missing?

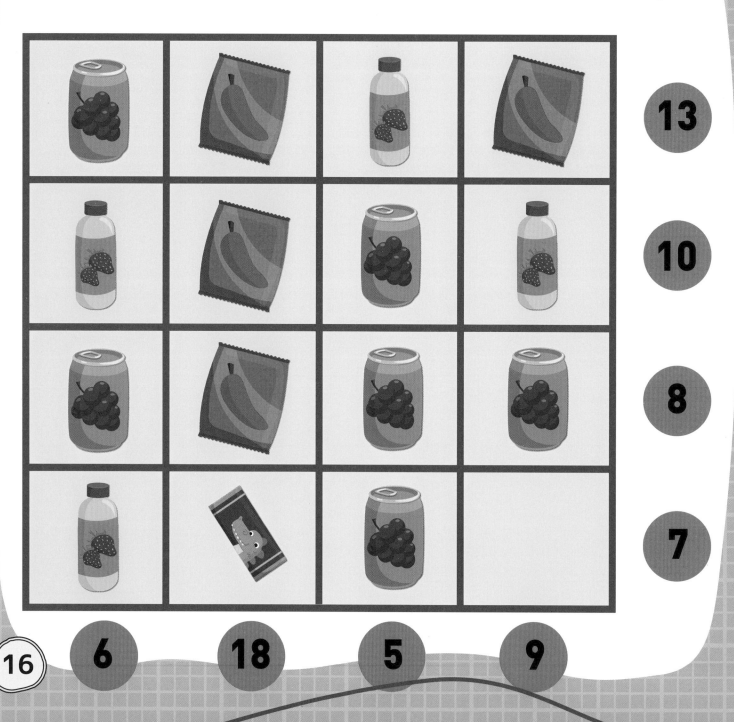

16

Karina owns 60 saris. 15% of them are green, and 24 of them are pink. One third of the remainder are yellow.

What percentage of her saris are pink?

How many of her saris are yellow?

Karina also has a fabulous collection of earrings! For her birthday, she receives 5 more pairs as gifts, but she gives away 10 pairs to a charity auction. That still leaves her with 20 pairs. How many pairs did she have before her birthday?

Don't be scared of the large numbers. Follow the pattern, and you can work them out without a calculator.

These are so easy that Daisy can do them standing on her head!

$$11 \times 11 = 121$$

$$111 \times 111 = 12321$$

$$1111 \times 1111 = 1234321$$

$$11111 \times 11111 = ?$$

$$111111 \times 111111 = ?$$

$$1111111 \times 1111111 = ?$$

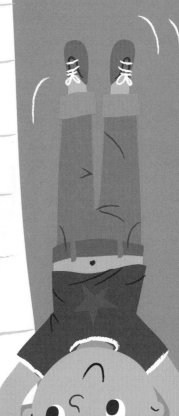

FAMILY VALUES

Dena is researching her family tree. Help her to figure out how old her relatives will be when she is 18, and some other questions that she wants to answer.

George Richards
born 1945

Faith Richards
born 1952

Kris Thompson
born 1949

Sally Thompson
born 1953

Peter Richards
born 1973

Megan Thompson
born 1977

Alyssa
born 2005

Dena
born 2008

AJ
born 2011

1. Which person was born 55 years before Dena?

2. How much younger than Dena is her brother?

3. At what age was Dena half the age of her sister?

PREDICTIONS

Each large square should contain two matching pairs of smaller squares. They can be any way up. Which small square is not needed to complete the patterns?

1

2

3

4

IN THE KITCHEN

CHOCOLATE CUPCAKES
Makes 16 cakes
1 1/3 cups flour
1/4 teaspoon baking soda
2 teaspoons baking powder
3/4 cup cocoa powder
3 tablespoons butter
1 1/2 cups sugar
2 eggs
3/4 teaspoon vanilla extract
1 3/4 cups milk

Sophia is busy today. She wants to make chocolate cupcakes for her friends.

1. How many cupcakes can she make with half a dozen eggs?

2. Why would it be difficult to make 24 chocolate cupcakes?

3. How much sugar would she need if she wants to make 32 cakes?

4. How many eggs will she use if she puts in 4 cups of flour?

LEAP PAD

Strike out the numbers that are divisible by 3 to leave a clear path for Freda to hop across.

36 93 54 43 36 9 28 60 52 18 48 39 10 16 37 15 22 63 12 45 73 6 57

Math-terpiece

Help Pablo Picatto finish his painting. Shade one third of all the triangles in purple, a half of the quadrilaterals in blue, and a quarter of the remaining shapes in pink.

A

B

C

Study the snake shapes. How many more snakes need to join in to make the next two patterns in the sequence?

How many snakes would there be if all five patterns were laid out together in full?

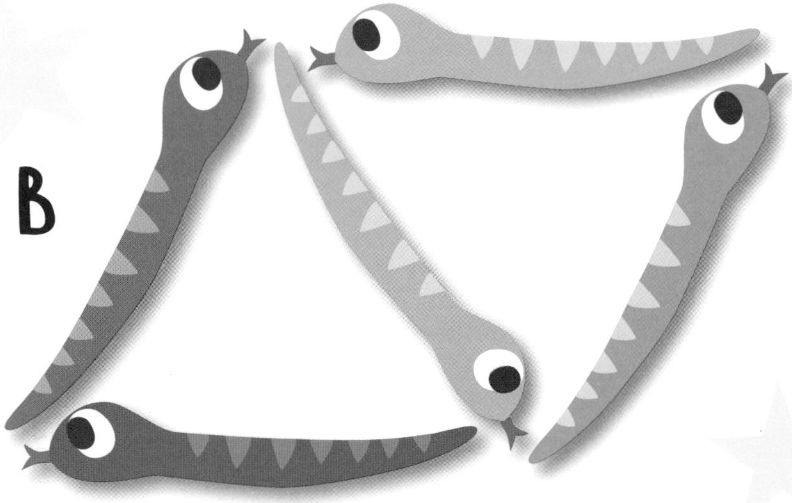

RIGHT ON CUE

Aaron, Bubba, Becca, and Maddie are playing pool. What is the highest number they can make by lining up all the balls on the table?

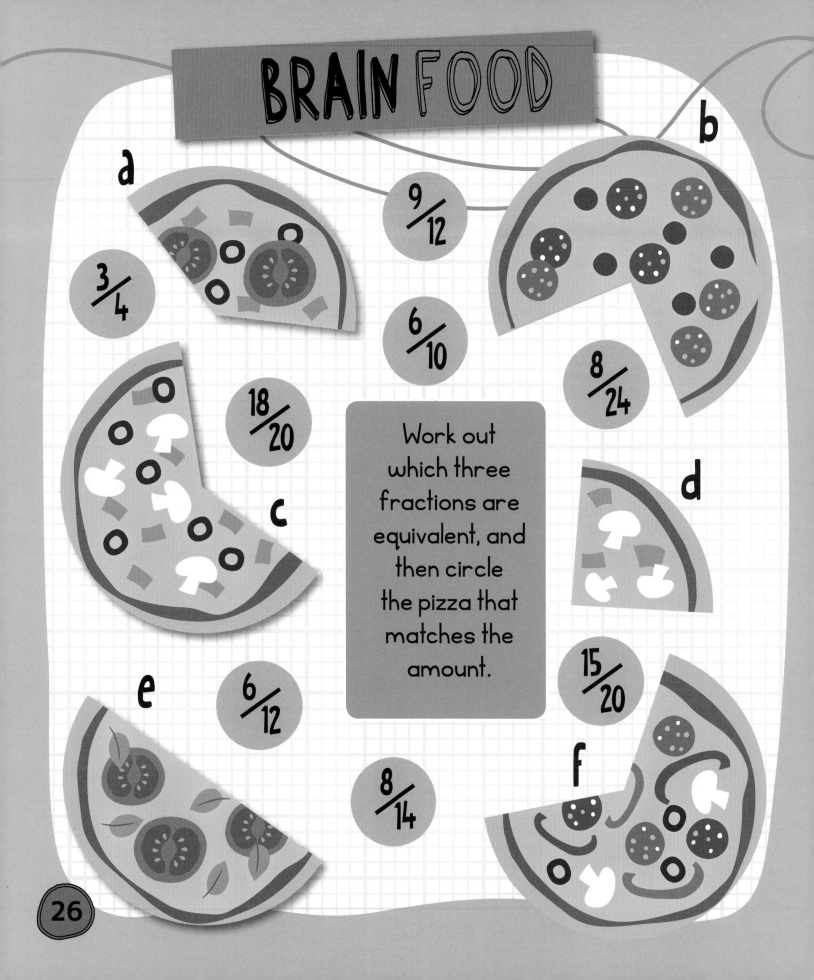

BRAIN FOOD

a

b

$\frac{9}{12}$

$\frac{3}{4}$

$\frac{6}{10}$

$\frac{8}{24}$

$\frac{18}{20}$

Work out which three fractions are equivalent, and then circle the pizza that matches the amount.

c

d

e

$\frac{6}{12}$

$\frac{15}{20}$

f

$\frac{8}{14}$

26

Alien encounter

Work out which of these aliens is the biggest by doing these calculations. Start with the problems in the brackets each time.

a $22 \div (4 \times 0.5)$

b $2 + (9 \times 2) - 6$

c $(16 \times 2) \div 4$

d $(18 \div 3) \times 2$

e $(8 \times 4) - (4 \times 4)$

f $(25 + 7) - 17$

WHERE IN THE WORLD?

Find out where Harriet is going, by working out the calculations, and matching the letters to the correct answers.

$G = 22 + 87$

$A = 139 - 15$

$R = 256 \div 2$

$F = 297 \div 3$

$S = 12^2$

$N = 52 \times 3$

$I = 77 \times 2$

$L = 155 - 23$

156	154	124	109	124	128	124

99	124	132	132	144

Get it right!

Ari wants to eat salmon and ginger, but not puffer fish. Which set menu should he choose?

Set menu 9

Set menu 24

Set menu 30

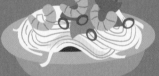

Set menu 15

Multiples of 5 contain puffer fish.

Multiples of 3 contain salmon.

Multiples of 2 contain ginger.

29

HOW STRIKING!

4

9

Wanda is adding a different number of lightning bolts to each cauldron, following a pattern. How many bolts should she put in the last cauldron?

14

19

Find a friend

Help each flamingo find a partner by matching the pairs that have the same answers.

32 ÷ 2

100 - 36

¹⁄₃ x 75

72 x 0.5

4 x 4

5 x 5

6 x 6

8 x 8

TIMES TABLE

Work out the answer to each puzzle using the code. Write the answers as numbers.

0   1   2   3   4   5   6   7   8   9

a) [egg] X [grapes] =

b) [cupcake] X [cupcake] =

c) [sandwich] X [meatball] =

d) [strawberry] X [cake] =

e) [cake] X [banana] =

f) [carrot] X [meatball] =

g) [meatball] X [grapes] =

h) [cake] X [egg] =

GREATER & LESSER

Add beaks to each of these penguins using the greater than and less than symbols > and < to make each statement correct. The first has been done to show you how.

a

14,293 > 14,263

b

528,653 ☐ 523,899

c

44,040 ☐ 44,404

d

792,099 ☐ 793,001

Summer sun

Here is a table showing where people went for their summer break.

☀ ☀ ☀	Boys	Girls	Total
The city	14		36
The mountains		18	
The beach	6		
Total	50		97

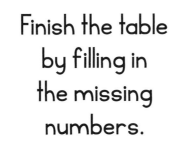

Finish the table by filling in the missing numbers.

SHOWBOTS

Which robot is holding up numbers that add up to exactly 99?

JIG-FIT

Rotate the jigsaw pieces to fit them into the puzzle. Which ones do not fit?

a

b

c

d

e

f

FRUIT TREATS

Malik has 3 packets of fruit chews to share between his party bags. Each packet contains 4 lime, 4 lemon, 4 orange, and 4 strawberry. He needs to make 7 party bags. Are there enough to put two of each fruit in every bag?

OUT OF THIS WORLD

Each of the planets has its own value, as shown.
Which of the rows or columns has the greatest total?

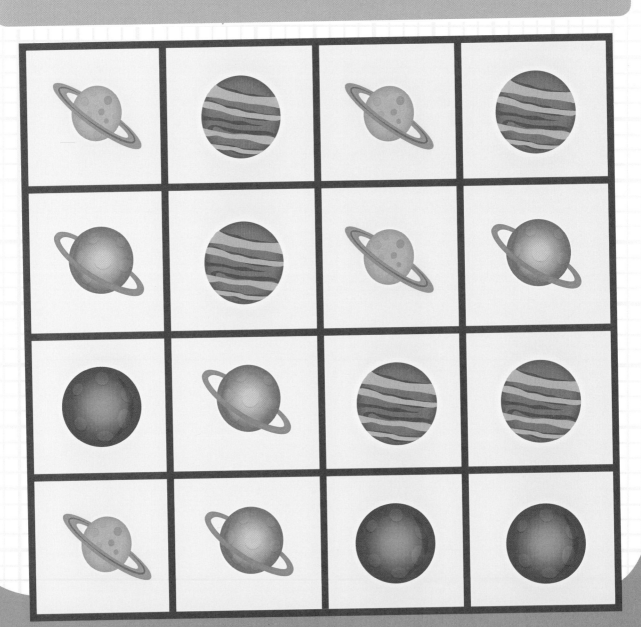

Ghost train

Suzy is waiting for her turn on the ghost train. Help her work out how long it will be before she gets on the ride.

The train has 12 carriages which each seat two people. The ride lasts for five minutes, with five minutes between rides for the changeover. Suzy counts 53 people in front of her. How long until her turn comes?

OH DEAR!

$$4 + (6 \times 4) = 28$$

$$4 \times 6 + 4 = 38$$

$$(4 + 6 \times 4) \times 2 = 56$$

$$(4 + 6) \times 4 = 40$$

$$(4 + 6 + 4) \times 4 = 56$$

Don't forget, do the problem
in the brackets first!

Oh dear, Mr. Dear! Which of the examples
on his board is incorrect?

Shining bright

How many of the items in Mr. Diamond's dazzling display have only a single line of symmetry?

FLYING HIGH

A jumbo jet holds 345 passengers. Fourteen are in first class, 52 are in club class, and the remainder are in economy seats.

a If 29 economy seats remain empty, and each economy passenger has a single piece of cabin luggage, how many bags are there in the economy section?

b Half of the first class passengers have two pieces of luggage. The other half have three pieces each. How many bags is that?

c 20% of the economy passengers have ordered a vegetarian meal. How many vegetarian trays should the cabin crew prepare?

Crab counters

Help the little octopus across the grid of crabs to reach his mother. He must follow the arrows to make a total of 15.

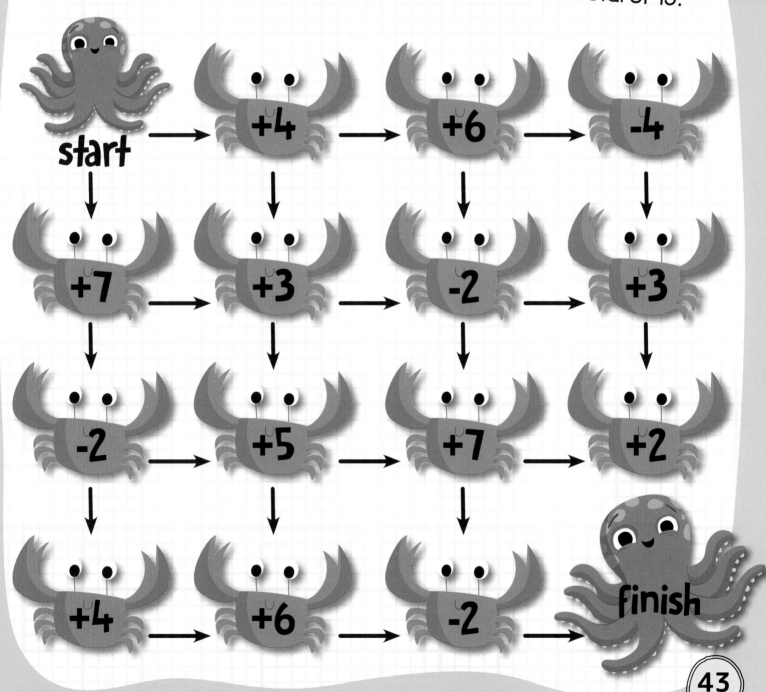

SNAKE PIT

Place three more snakes into the top grid so that
no snake is in the same row, column,
or diagonal as another snake.

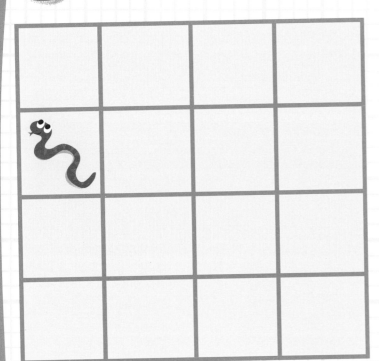

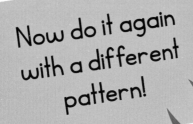

Now do it again
with a different
pattern!

You need to move from corner to corner, but should you choose the pink route or the yellow route? Which one will give you a positive score rather than a negative score?

-5
+2
+3
+1

OFF COURSE

a

Three of these rockets are heading in the right direction, but one has set the wrong co-ordinates. Do the calculations to work out the rocket which is heading in a different direction.

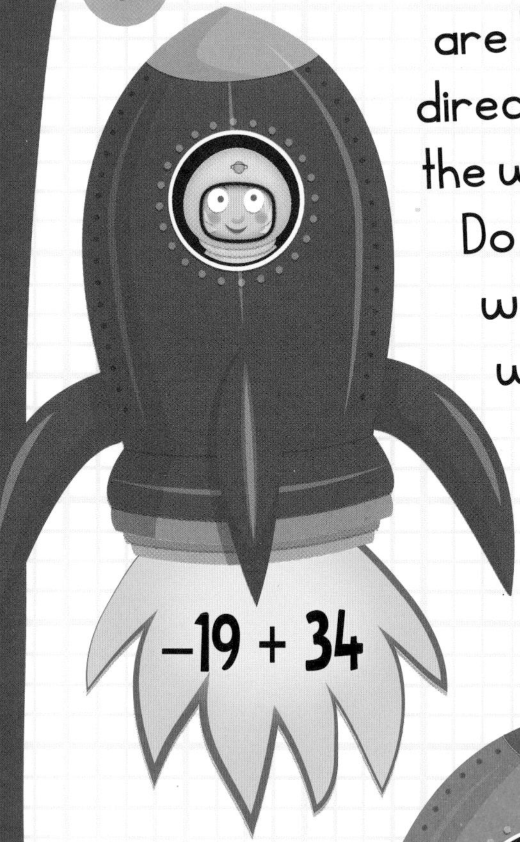

b

−19 + 34

160 ÷ 5

c

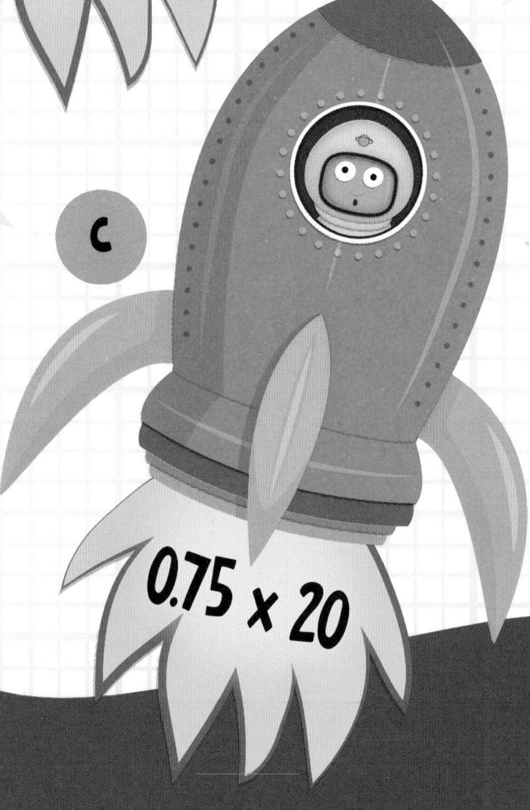

0.75 x 20

d

46 − 31

Each hummingbird drinks from a flower with a number equal to its own number.

3^2

7^2

5^2

25   36   49

Which bird has no flower, and which flower has no bird?

It takes time

Trudi's clock is five minutes slow. She has to get ready for a party at 4pm. Will she make it on time?

Trudi takes 15 minutes to dry her hair.

She needs 10 minutes to put on her make up.

It is a 30-minute journey from her home to the party.

Don't forget: the clock is a mirror image!

ARCHITECT'S ANGLES

Study the diagram and work out the missing angles a, b, and c.

Remember:

Angles inside a quadrilateral add up to 360°

Angles inside a triangle add up to 180°

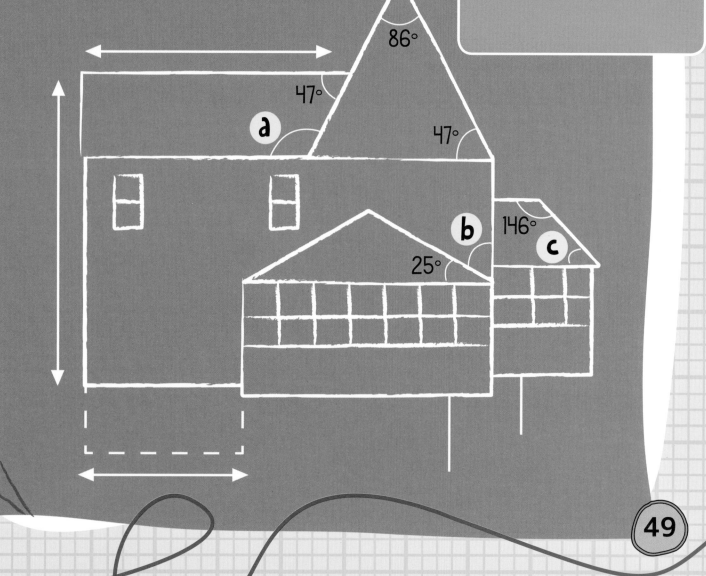

ON DISPLAY

Ewan arranges his football cards in his album. Each page has 4 rows of cards with 3 cards in each row.

How many pages will 135 cards take up? How many will be on the last, incomplete, page?

Fish figures

Work out which number is represented by each symbol to make the sums add up on each row and column. The numbers are 4, 5, 7, and 10.

IN A HOLE

The monster is stuck in a hole that is 30 times his own height. Every minute he climbs three times his own height, but falls back twice his own height. How many minutes does it take him to get out of the hole?

LAB TEST

x4 =28

÷10 =___

x12 =__

x0.5

x8

÷2

x1.1

x5

x6

x3

7

Sadie the scientist mixes each chemical with the pink liquid she's holding. Fill in the missing numbers to show what happens! The first one has been filled in for you.

WAKEY WAKEY!

Help Sanjay work out the solutions to these problems, so that he doesn't miss anything important! Use the 24-hour clock for your answers.

Sanjay sets his alarm for 07:00. It tells him that it is set for 9 hours and 27 minutes from the current time. What time is it now?

He must get up before 07:30. If his alarm waits for 8 minutes each time he presses the snooze button, how many times can he press it before getting up?

07:00

Sanjay eats breakfast at 07:42, and leaves the house thirty-six minutes after that. What time does he close the door behind him?

PARTY PUNCH

Maya makes fruit punch with 3 cartons of apple juice, 2 bottles of fizzy water, and 4 cartons of cranberry juice.

This combination makes 20 servings of punch.
How many servings can she make with 4.5 cartons of apple juice, 3 bottles of fizzy water, and 6 cartons of cranberry?
How many cartons of cranberry are needed to make 100 servings?

TILE TROUBLE

Brian the builder has to lay a set of tiles. Help him work out how to fill the space using all of the tiles.

Hint:
The tiles are double sided, so they can be rotated or reversed.

Each number in the sequence is made by adding the previous two numbers together. Can you fill in the gaps?

a. 4 — 7 — — — —

b. 3 — 6 — — — —

c. — 8 — 12 — — —

d. 6 — — 10 — 24

GONE WITH THE WIND

A tree has 8,192 leaves on day 1. If half of the leaves are blown off every day, on what day will there be just one leaf left?

NUMBER TREE

Which three numbers fill the spaces just above the tree trunk? Each number is the total of the two numbers below it.

99

43

18   25

12   13   18

4

ARE YOU SHORE?

Find a route across the beach that equals 20, adding as you travel in the direction of the arrows. Is 20 the largest total you can make?

4 → 9 → 2

start → 9 → 7 → 1 → finish

6 → 3 → 5

Positive thinking

Follow each route from corner to corner, adding up the score. Which path, pink or yellow, gives a positive score?

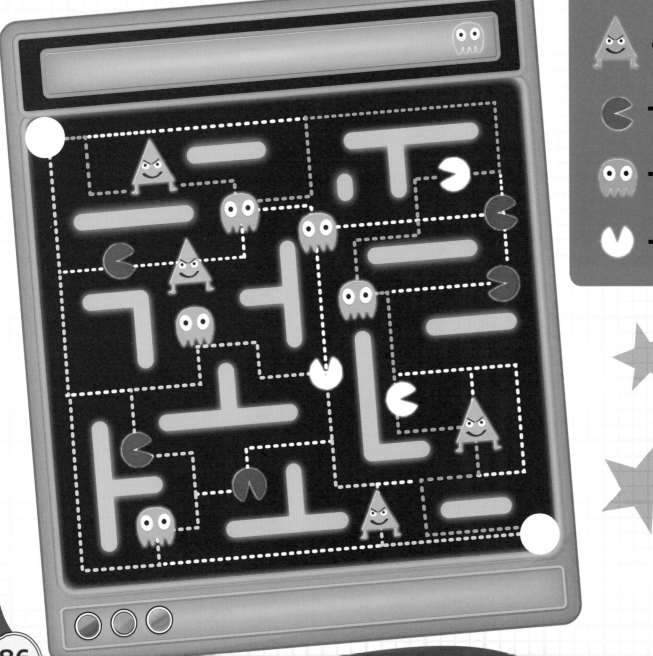

 -5

 +2

 +3

 +1

A stickie situation

Becca and Maddie are marking up a book for revision. The book has 48 pages. Work out the answers to the questions below.

They put a pink stickie note on every page with a factor of 7. They mark every page with a factor of 4 in green. Yellow notes go on all the pages with a factor of 3.

a) How many pages have just 2 stickie notes?

b) How many pages have no notes?

c) How many pages have 3 stickie notes?

HAT TRICK

Help Wanda Witch work out the answer. No magic required, just a little bit of lateral thinking!

How many times bigger than the small hat is the large hat?

88

LASER LIGHTS

Sadie is experimenting with lasers. Her first setup has 4 laser beams, as shown. It has one intersecting point.

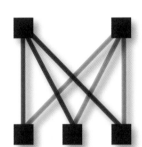

She adds two more laser beams aimed at an extra target, creating 3 intersecting points, like this.

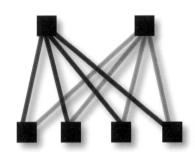

Another two laser beams aimed at an additional target gives 6 intersecting points.

Fill in the table to work out how many intersecting points there will be if there are 10 targets.

Number of points at the bottom	Number of intersections
2	1
3	3
4	6
5	10

Answers

4. Race against time

It is now 1:30pm, and the sculpture shown will take 3 hours and 35 minutes. So it will be finished at 5:05, giving 1 hour 25 minutes for people to see the finished sculpture.

5. Parking space

1 truck and 2 cars will have to park elsewhere.

6. Best in show

Gold cup = 8
Red rosette = 10
Orange rosette = 7

7. Monster munch

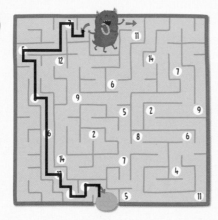

8. T-shirt trends

1. 6 stars
2. 100 stars
3. Long sleeves (it's an even number)
4. 31 spots

9. Snack time

100 frogs
1,000 crickets
10,000 blades of grass

10. Sail away

Ship 39

11. Hungry games

30 minutes
6 caterpillars eat 10 leaves each in an hour. So 8 caterpillars would eat 80 leaves in an hour, or 40 leaves in half that time.

12. Gift wrapped

5 (Numbers 1, 3, and 4 don't fold into a cube. Numbers 2 and 6 don't have the patterns in the correct place.)

13. Toy cars

2. 1/4
3. 2/5
4. 1/3
5. 1/4

14. Brain block

26

15. Deck the halls

Cut the last two flags off strings A and D and swap them over. Cut strings B and D in half and swap them over. This will give you:

516342
564321
245136
132654

16. Sneaky snacks

Grape juice is missing.

17. Movie star

40% are pink. 9 are yellow.
She had 25 pairs of earrings.

18. Upsy daisy

11111 × 11111 = 123454321
111111 × 111111 = 12345654321
1111111 × 1111111 = 1234567654321

19. Family values

Dena will be 18 in 2026. These are the ages of her relatives in that year:
George Richards 81   Faith Richards 74
Kris Thompson 77   Sally Thompson 73
Peter Richards 53   Megan Thompson 49
Alyssa 21   AJ 15
1. Sally Thompson was born 55 years before Dena.
2. Her brother is 3 years younger.
3. Age 3 (Dena) and 6 (Alyssa).

20. Predictions

2

21. In the kitchen

1. 48
2. She will need to increase the ingredients by half as much again, which is tricky with 1 1/3 cups of flour and 3/4 teaspoon vanilla extract.
3. 3 cups
4. 6 eggs

22. Leap pad

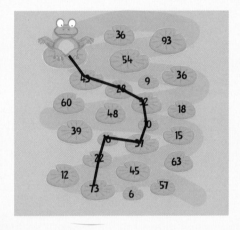

23. Math-terpiece

You can shade them in your own pattern, but you should have 4 purple triangles, 8 blue quadrilaterals, and 4 pink shapes.

24. Snakes alive!

4 snakes complete the next two patterns. Altogether you would need 35 snakes.

25. Right on cue

954,321

26. Brain food
3/4 = 9/12 = 15/20, seen on pizza b

27. Alien encounter
Alien e is the biggest.
a. 11
b. 14
c. 8
d. 12
e. 16
f. 15

28. Where in the world?
NIAGARA FALLS

29. Get it right!
Set menu 24

30. How striking!
She adds 5 lightning bolts to give:
4 9 14 19 24

31. Find a friend
$32 \div 2 = 4 \times 4$
$1/3 \times 75 = 5 \times 5$
$72 \times 0.5 = 6 \times 6$
$100 - 36 = 8 \times 8$

32. Times table
a. 56   b. 9
c. 30   d. 36
e. 18   f. 0
g. 35   h. 72

33. Greater and lesser
a. > b. > c. < d. <

34. Summer sun

	Boys	Girls	Total
The city	14	22	36
The mountains	30	18	48
The beach	6	7	13
Total	50	47	97

35. Showbots
e

36. Jig-fit
b, d, f

37. Fruit treats
No! There are 12 of each fruit, and he needs 14 of each to fill 7 bags with 2 per bag.

38. Out of this world
The bottom row adds up to 16, which is more than any other row or column.

39. Ghost train
20 minutes (she will be on the third ride, and the previous two rides will take 10 minutes each).

40. Oh dear!
$4 \times 6 + 4 = 38$ is incorrect

41. Shining bright

42. Flying high
a. 250 b. 35 c. 50

43. Crab counters

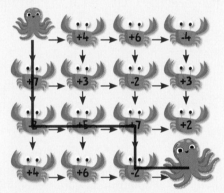

44. Snake pit
Here are two possible solutions:

45. High score
The pink route

46. Off course
b

47. Beautiful birds
Bird 3^2 has no flower. Flower 36 has no bird.

48. It takes time
Yes, with 20 minutes to spare.

49. Architect's angles
a. 133° b. 65° c. 34°

50. On display
12 pages, with just 3 cards on the last page.

51. Fish figures

star = 4   fish = 5

jellyfish = 7   shell = 10

52. In a hole
28 minutes. After 27 minutes he has just three times his height left to climb, which takes him to the top and he gets out.

53. Lab test
$7 \times 4 = 28$
$7 \div 10 = 0.7$
$7 \times 12 = 84$
$7 \times 0.5 = 3.5$
$7 \times 8 = 56$
$7 \div 2 = 3.5$
$7 \times 1.1 = 7.7$
$7 \times 5 = 35$
$7 \times 6 = 42$
$7 \times 3 = 21$

54. Wakey wakey!
The time now is 21:33.
He can press snooze 3 times.
He closes the door at 08:18.

55. Party punch
30 servings; 20 cartons of cranberry

56. Tile trouble
Here is one
possible
solution:

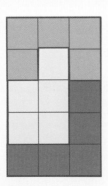

57. Frightfully simple
a. 4 7 11 18 29
b. 3 6 9 15 24
c. 4 8 12 20 32
d. 6 4 10 14 24

58. Pumpkin patch
CJ picks the most.

59. Koala counting

60. Seven seashells
Here is one
possible
solution:

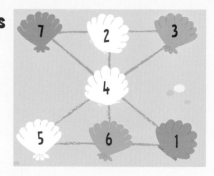

61. Super science

62. Car capers

63. Light up my life
10 lanterns

64. Tree top
77

65. On the shelf
15 books per shelf. Shelf 1 has C at the end,
shelf 2 has P, shelf 3 has W.

66. Flower show
30 bricks

67. Rabbits on the run

12 minutes (it is the first number that can be divided by 1, 2, 3, and 4)

68. Penguin path

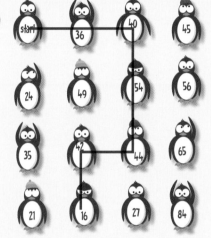

69. Casting a spell

15 in the top cauldron, and 5 in the bottom cauldron.

70. Head scratcher

2 + 2 + 2 = 6

3 x 3 - 3 = 6

5 ÷ 5 + 5 = 6

6 + 6 - 6 = 6

7 ÷ 7 + 7 = 6

71. Twinkle twinkle

2, 4, 5, 7

72. Elementary

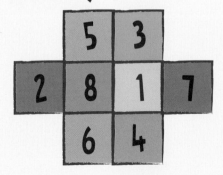

73. Mole hole

1/4. This is why: Each mole can travel in two directions, so there are 2 x 2 x 2 (= 8) possible ways they can crawl altogether. If all the moles crawl in the same (eg clockwise) direction, they won't meet. If all the moles crawl in the opposite direction, they won't meet. That means that 2 out of a possible 8 (or 1/4) are scenarios where they won't bump into another mole.

74. Pencil problem

This is one efficient way, but you might have found another!

75. Car share

5 (3 cars have both. 3 cars have a passenger only in the front (6 - 3 = 3) and 1 has a passenger only in the back (4 - 3 = 1). That makes 7 cars with passengers somewhere (3 + 3 + 1 = 7) leaving 5 of the 12 cars with no passenger.

76. Eggs-actly!

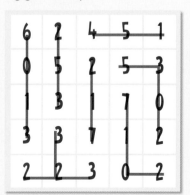

77. Family album

She should start with a full-page picture, ending with 2 small ones and half a blank page.

78. Bee lines

Here is one possible solution.

79. Eating eights

20 times (10 numbers end in 8, and 10 more numbers begin with 8).

80. As easy as 123

Here is one way:
2 1 3
3 2 1
1 3 2

81. More tile trouble

Here is one possible solution.

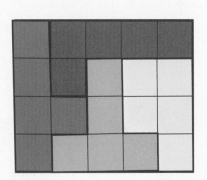

82. Keep fit

1. 6
2. 8
3. 5
4. 26
5. 3

83. Gone with the wind

Day 14

84. Number tree

2 10 3

85. Are you shore?

9 + 9 + 2 = 20
The largest total is 9 + 7 + 5 = 21

86. Positive thinking

The yellow route

87. A stickie situation

a. 7 b. 21 c. None

88. Hat trick

It is four times bigger. You don't need any measurements to work it out. If you imagine rotating the small hat inside the circle you will make this shape. Now it is easy to see that the small hat is one quarter the size of the large hat.

89. Laser lights

Number of points at the bottom	Number of intersections
2	1
3	3
4	6
5	10
6	15
7	21
8	28
9	36
10	45